Montessori SPANISH WORKBOOK

Montessori Spanish Workbook
© Kyra Starr. All rights reserved.

Translations: Luiz Fernando Peters

No part of this publication may be reproduced, distributed, or transmitted, in any form or by any means, including photocopying, recording, or other electronic or mechanical methods, without prior written permission of the publisher, except in the case of brief quotations embodied in critical reviews and certain other noncommercial uses permitted by copyright law.

This book belongs to

Name: _____   Date: _____

Spanish
Number Matching

Directions: Match the numbers to their Spanish counterparts.

1	2	3	4

Uno

Dos
Two

Tres

Cuatro
Four

Uno
One

Dos

Tres
Three

Cuatro

Name: _____ Date: _____

Spanish
Number Matching

Directions: Match the numbers to their Spanish counterparts.

5	6	7	8

Cinco

Seis
Six

Siete

Ocho
Eight

Cinco
Five

Seis

Siete
Seven

Ocho

Name: _____ Date: _____

Spanish
Number Matching

Directions: Match the numbers to their Spanish counterparts.

9	10	11	12

✂----------------------

Nueve	Diez Ten	Once	Doce Twelve
Nueve Nine	Diez	Once Eleven	Doce

Name: _____ Date: _____

Spanish
Number Matching

Directions: Match the numbers to their Spanish counterparts.

13	14	15	16

Trece

Catorce
Fourteen

Quince

Dieciséis
Sixteen

Trece
Thirteen

Catorce

Quince
Fifteen

Dieciséis

Name: _____ Date: _____

Spanish
Number Matching

Directions: Match the numbers to their Spanish counterparts.

17	18	19	20

Diecisiete

Dieciocho
Eighteen

Diecinueve

Veinte
Twenty

Diecisiete
Seventeen

Dieciocho

Diecinueve
Nineteen

Veinte

Parts of a Flower
partes de una flor

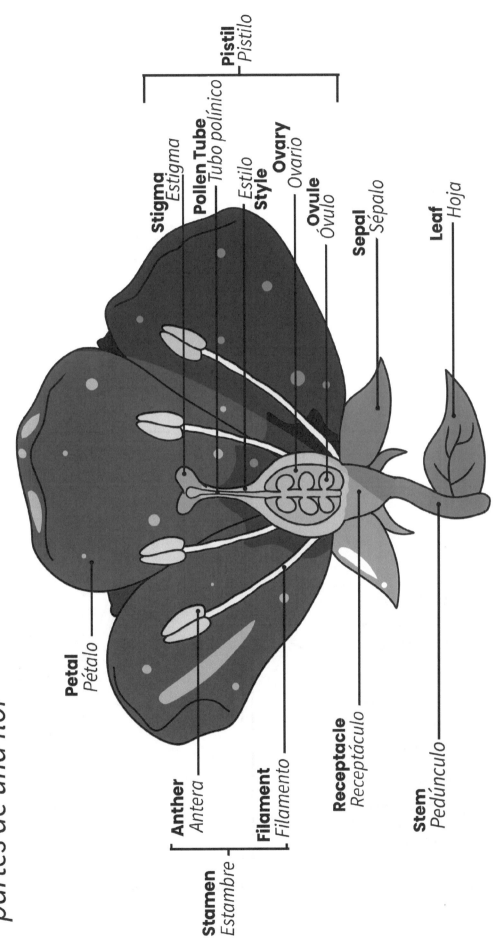

Estilo
Style

Estilo
Style

Estigma
Stigma

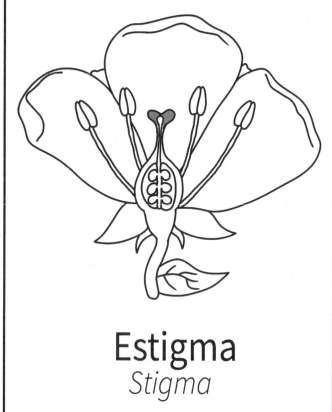

Estigma
Stigma

Pedúnculo
Stem

Pedúnculo
Stem

Estambre
Stamen

Estambre
Stamen

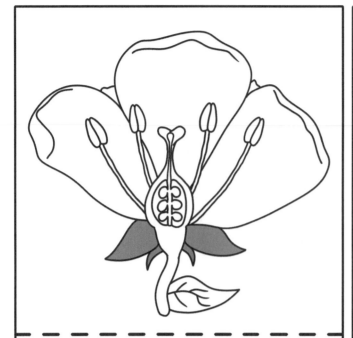

Sépalo
Sepal

Sépalo
Sepal

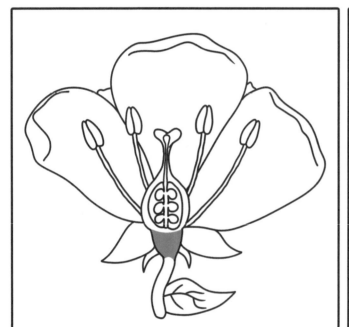

Receptáculo
Receptacle

Receptáculo
Receptacle

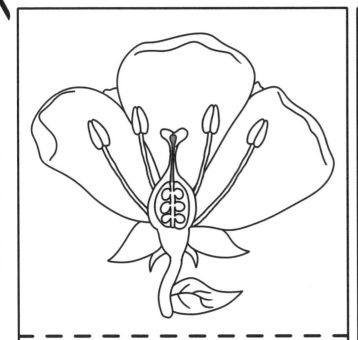

Tubo polínico
Pollen Tube

Tubo polínico
Pollen Tube

Pistilo
Pistil

Pistilo
Pistil

Pétalo
Petal

Pétalo
Petal

Óvulo
Ovule

Óvulo
Ovule

Ovario
Ovary

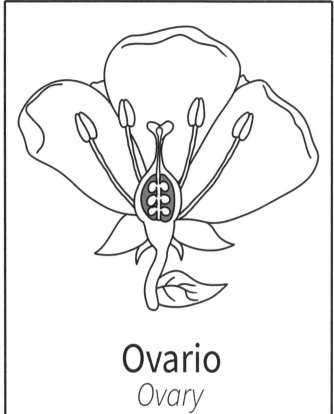

Ovario
Ovary

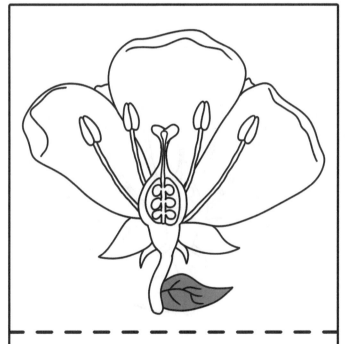

Hoja
Leaf

Hoja
Leaf

Flor
Flower

Flor
Flower

Filamento
Filament

Filamento
Filament

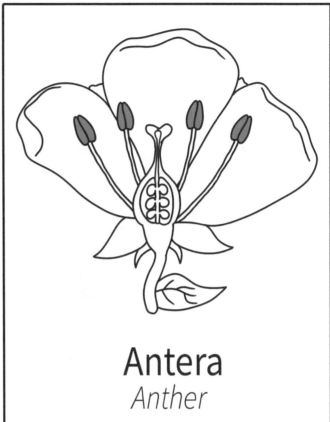

Antera
Anther

Antera
Anther

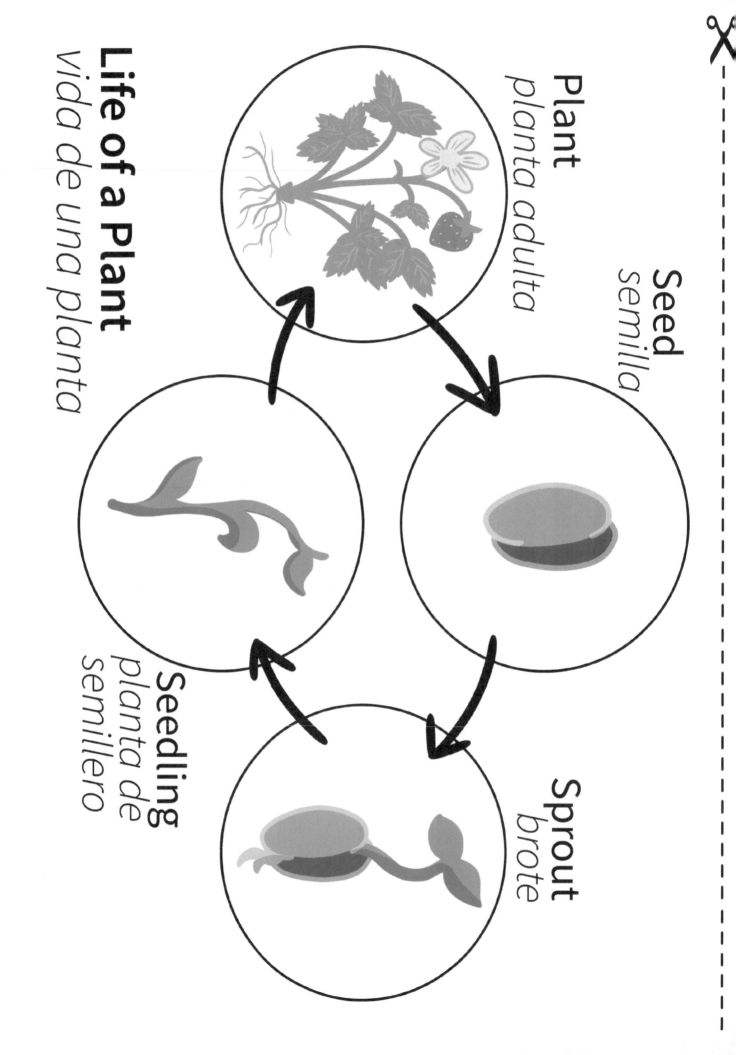

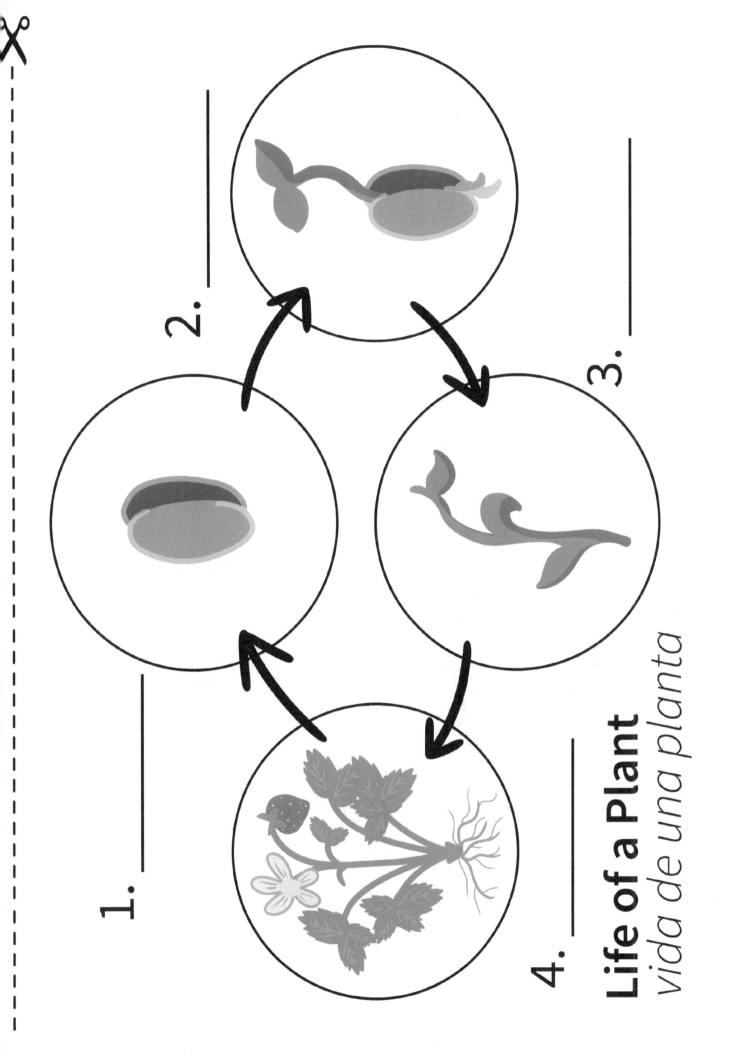

Life of a Plant
vida de una planta

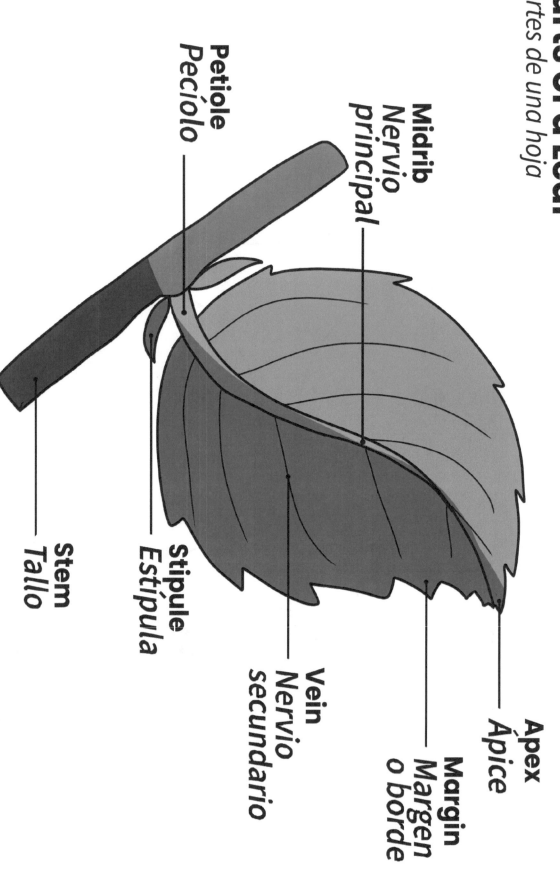

Nervio secundario
Veins

Estípula
Stipule

Tallo
Stem

Pecíolo
Petiole

Nervio principal
Midrib

Margen o borde
Margin

Hoja
Leaf

Ápice
Apex

Parts of a Plant
partes de una planta

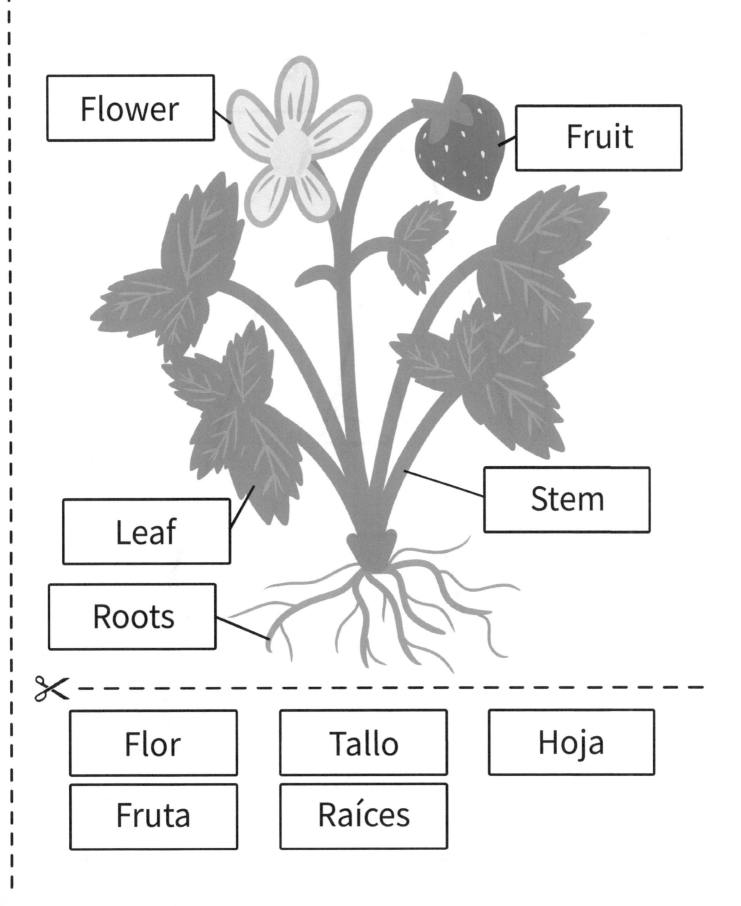

Name: _____ Date: _____

Spanish
Color the Alphabet

Avestruz
Ostrich

Name: _____ Date: _____

Spanish
Color the Alphabet

Name: _____ Date: _____

Spanish
Color the Alphabet

Carpincho
Capybara

Name: _____ Date: _____

Spanish
Color the Alphabet

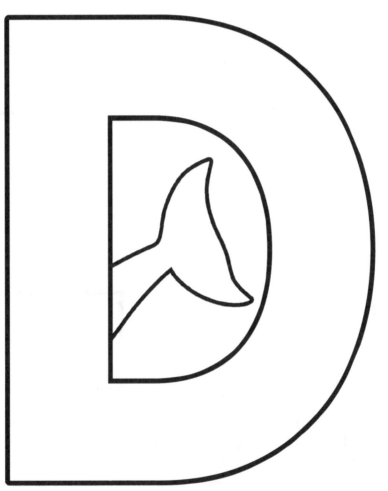

Name: _____ Date: _____

Spanish
Color the Alphabet

Elefante
Elephant

Name: _____ Date: _____

Spanish
Color the Alphabet

Flor
Flower

Name: _____ **Date:** _____

Spanish
Color the Alphabet

Gato
Cat

Name: _____ Date: _____

Spanish
Color the Alphabet

Hipopótamo
Hippopotamus

Name: _____ **Date:** _____

Spanish
Color the Alphabet

Iguana
Iguana

Name: _____ Date: _____

Spanish
Color the Alphabet

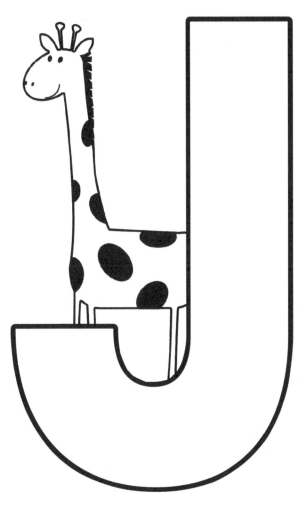

Jirafa
Giraffe

Name: _____   Date: _____

Spanish
Color the Alphabet

Kiwi
Kiwi

Name: _____ Date: _____

Spanish
Color the Alphabet

León
Lion

Name: _____ Date: _____

Spanish
Color the Alphabet

Mono
Monkey

Name: _____ Date: _____

Spanish
Color the Alphabet

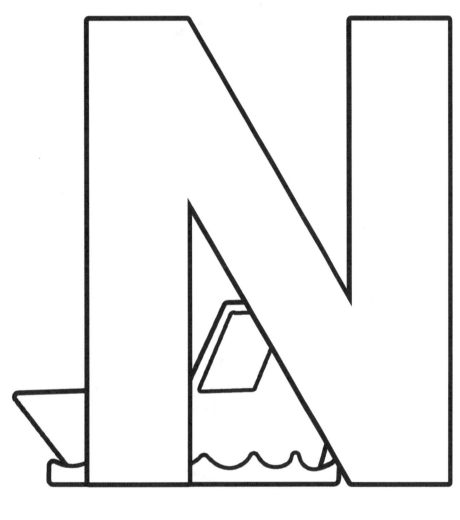

Nave
Ship

Name: _____ Date: _____

Spanish
Color the Alphabet

Oveja
Sheep

Name: _____   **Date:** _____

Spanish
Color the Alphabet

Pato
Duck

Name: _____ **Date:** _____

Spanish
Color the Alphabet

Name: _____ **Date:** _____

Spanish
Color the Alphabet

Ratón
Mouse

Name: _____ **Date:** _____

Spanish
Color the Alphabet

Name: _____ Date: _____

Spanish
Color the Alphabet

Tigre
Tiger

Name: _____ Date: _____

Spanish
Color the Alphabet

Uvas
Grapes

Name: _____ Date: _____

Spanish
Color the Alphabet

Vaca
Cow

Name: _____ **Date:** _____

Spanish
Color the Alphabet

Wok
Wok

Name: _____ Date: _____

Spanish
Color the Alphabet

Xilófono
Xylophone

Name: _____ Date: _____

Spanish
Color the Alphabet

Yedra
Ivy

Name: _____ Date: _____

Spanish
Color the Alphabet

Zanahoria
Carrot

Name: _____ Date: _____

Identifying Weather

Identify the word in Spanish and draw it in the box below.

Ventoso

Name: _____ Date: _____

Identifying Weather

Identify the word in Spanish and draw it in the box below.

Soleado

Name: _____ **Date:** _____

Identifying Weather

Identify the word in Spanish and draw it in the box below.

Tormentoso

Name: _____ Date: _____

Identifying Weather

Identify the word in Spanish and draw it in the box below.

Nieva

Name: _____ Date: _____

Identifying Weather

Identify the word in Spanish and draw it in the box below.

Lluvioso

Name: _____ Date: _____

Identifying Weather

Identify the word in Spanish and draw it in the box below.

Arcoíris

Name: _____ Date: _____

Identifying Weather

Identify the word in Spanish and draw it in the box below.

Parcialmente Nublado

Name: _____ Date: _____

Identifying Weather

Identify the word in Spanish and draw it in the box below.

Neblinoso

Name: _____ **Date:** _____

Identifying Weather

Identify the word in Spanish and draw it in the box below.

Nublado

Ventoso
Windy

Cálido
Warm

Soleado
Sunny

Tormentoso
Stormy

Ventoso
Windy

Cálido
Warm

Soleado
Sunny

Tormentoso
Stormy

Nieva
Snowing

Lluvioso
Rainy

Arcoíris
Rainbow

Parcialmente Nublado
Partly Cloudy

Nieva
Snowing

Lluvioso
Rainy

Arcoíris
Rainbow

Parcialmente Nublado
Partly Cloudy

Calor
Hot

Neblinoso
Foggy

Frío
Cold

Nublado
Cloudy

Name: _____ Date: _____

Where is Spanish spoken?

Directions: Draw and color the flag, then trace the word below.

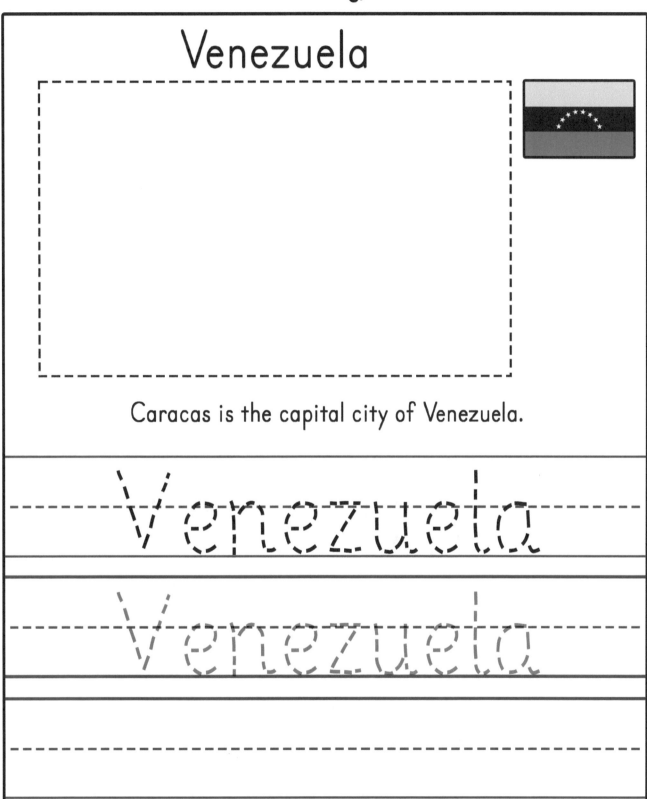

Venezuela

Caracas is the capital city of Venezuela.

Venezuela

Venezuela

Name: _____ Date: _____

Where is Spanish spoken?

Directions: Draw and color the flag, then trace the word below.

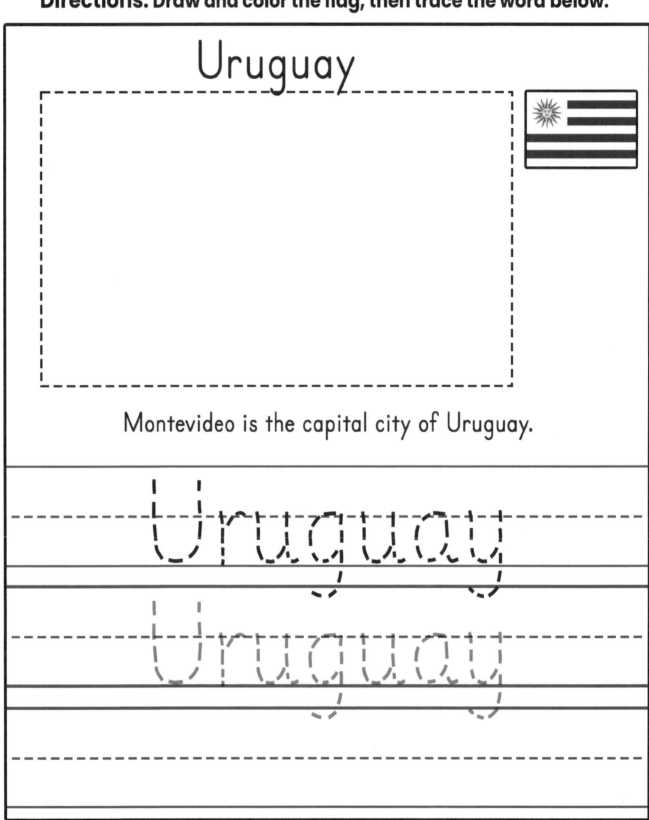

Uruguay

Montevideo is the capital city of Uruguay.

Uruguay

Uruguay

Name: _____ Date: _____

Where is Spanish spoken?

Directions: Draw and color the flag, then trace the word below.

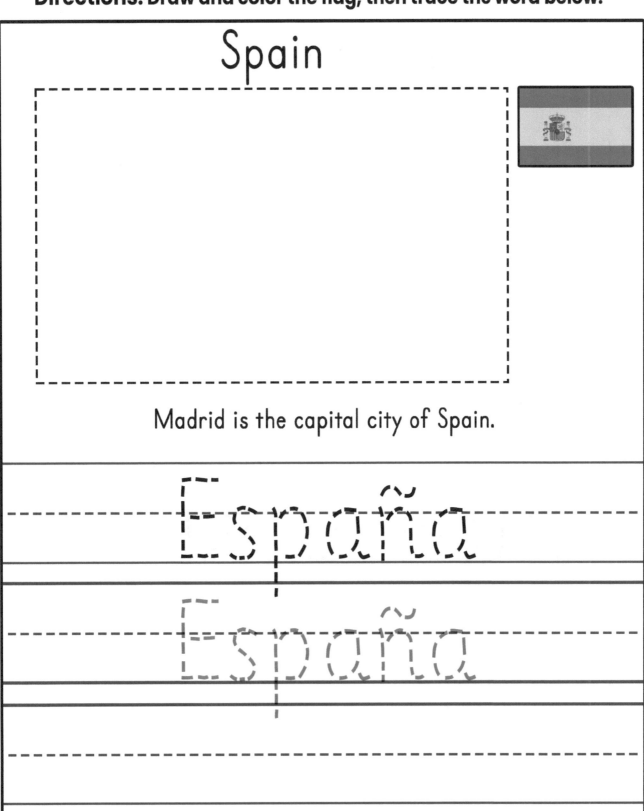

Spain

Madrid is the capital city of Spain.

España

España

Name: _____ Date: _____

Where is Spanish spoken?

Directions: Draw and color the flag, then trace the word below.

Puerto Rico

San Juan is the capital city of Puerto Rico.

Puerto Rico

Puerto Rico

Name: _____ Date: _____

Where is Spanish spoken?

Directions: Draw and color the flag, then trace the word below.

Peru

Lima is the capital city of Peru.

Perú

Perú

Name: _____ Date: _____

Where is Spanish spoken?

Directions: Draw and color the flag, then trace the word below.

Paraguay

Asunción is the capital city of Paraguay.

Paraguay

Paraguay

Name: _____ Date: _____

Where is Spanish spoken?

Directions: Draw and color the flag, then trace the word below.

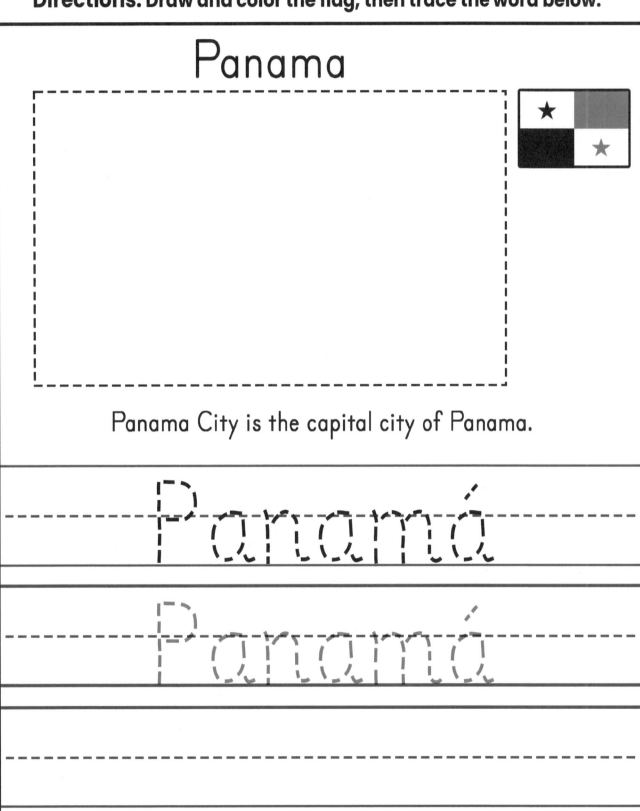

Name: _____ Date: _____

Where is Spanish spoken?

Directions: Draw and color the flag, then trace the word below.

Name: _____ Date: _____

Where is Spanish spoken?

Directions: Draw and color the flag, then trace the word below.

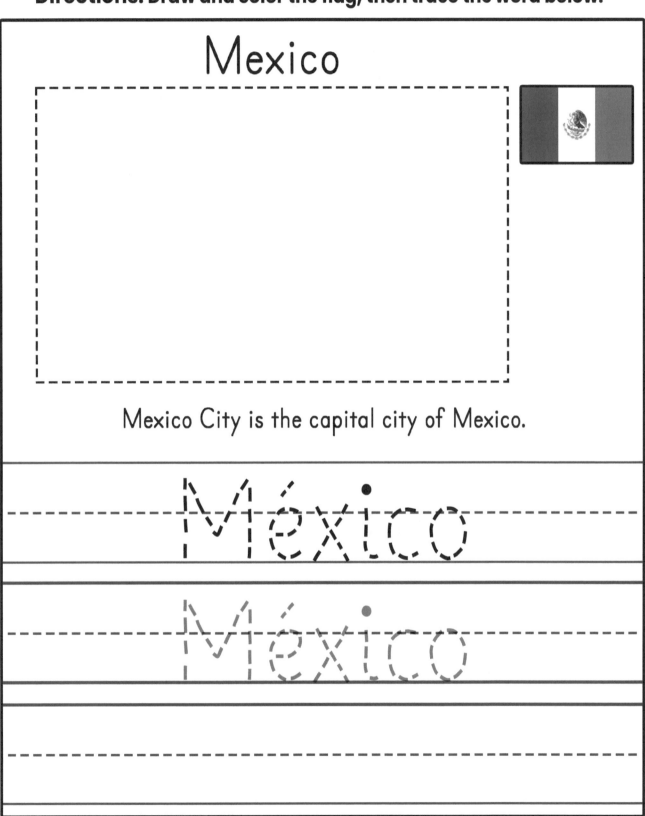

Mexico

Mexico City is the capital city of Mexico.

México

México

Name: _____ Date: _____

Where is Spanish spoken?

Directions: Draw and color the flag, then trace the word below.

Honduras

Tegucigalpa is the capital city of Honduras.

Honduras

Honduras

Name: _____ Date: _____

Where is Spanish spoken?

Directions: Draw and color the flag, then trace the word below.

Name: _____ Date: _____

Where is Spanish spoken?

Directions: Draw and color the flag, then trace the word below.

Equatorial Guinea

Malabo is the capital city of Equatorial Guinea.

Equatorial
Guinea

Name: _____ Date: _____

Where is Spanish spoken?

Directions: Draw and color the flag, then trace the word below.

Name: _____ Date: _____

Where is Spanish spoken?

Directions: Draw and color the flag, then trace the word below.

Ecuador

Quito is the capital city of Ecuador.
(formally San Francisco de Quito)

Ecuador

Ecuador

Name: _____ Date: _____

Where is Spanish spoken?

Directions: Draw and color the flag, then trace the word below.

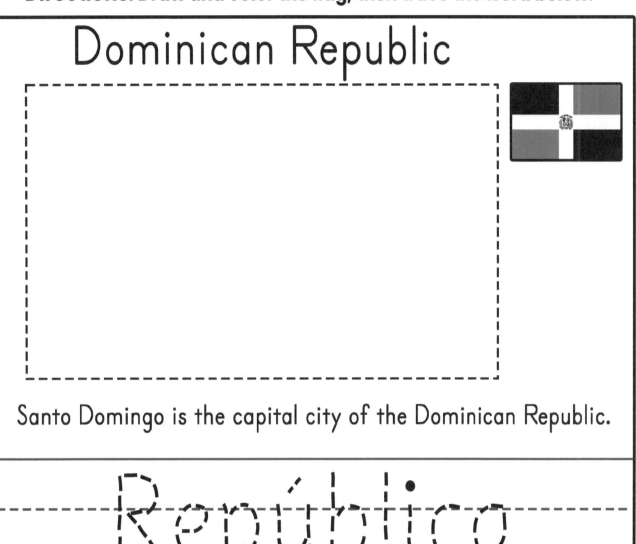

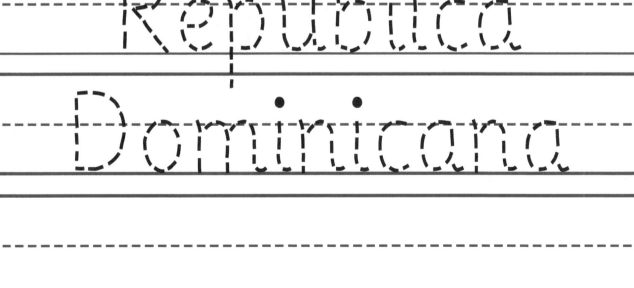

Name: _____ Date: _____

Where is Spanish spoken?

Directions: Draw and color the flag, then trace the word below.

Cuba

Havana is the capital city of Cuba.

Cuba

Cuba

Name: _____ Date: _____

Where is Spanish spoken?

Directions: Draw and color the flag, then trace the word below.

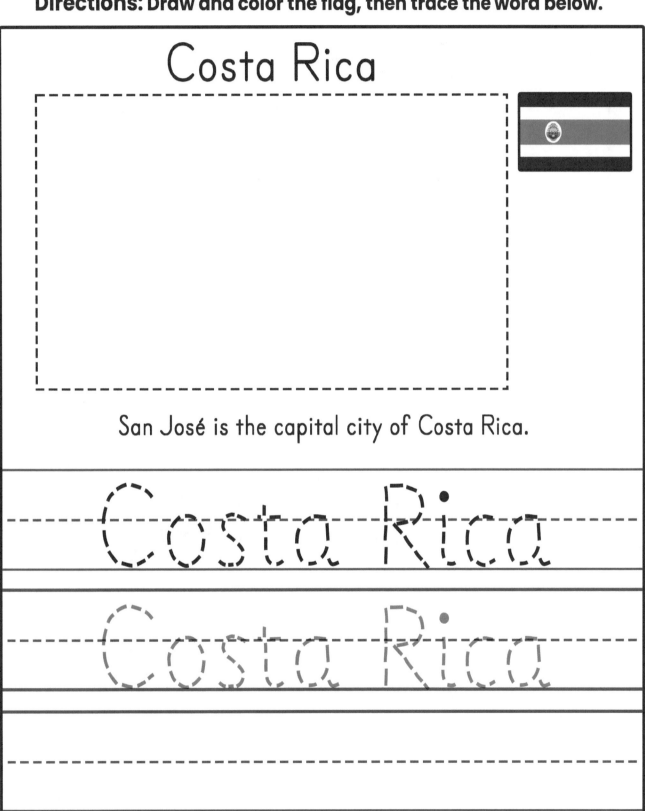

Costa Rica

San José is the capital city of Costa Rica.

Costa Rica

Costa Rica

Name: _____ Date: _____

Where is Spanish spoken?

Directions: Draw and color the flag, then trace the word below.

Colombia

Bogotá is the capital city of Colombia.

Colombia

Colombia

Name: _____ Date: _____

Where is Spanish spoken?

Directions: Draw and color the flag, then trace the word below.

Chile

Santiago is the capital city of Chile.

Chile

Chile

Name: _____ **Date:** _____

Where is Spanish spoken?

Directions: Draw and color the flag, then trace the word below.

Name: _____ Date: _____

Where is Spanish spoken?

Directions: Draw and color the flag, then trace the word below.

Argentina

Buenos Aires is the capital city of Argentina.

Argentina

Argentina

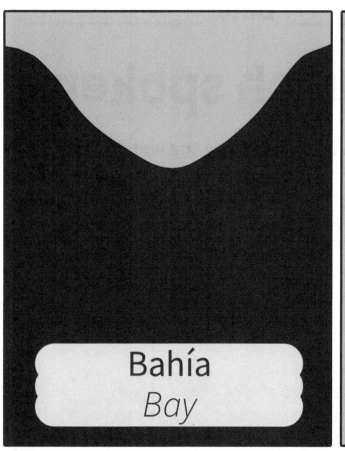

Bahía
Bay

Archipiélago
Archipelago

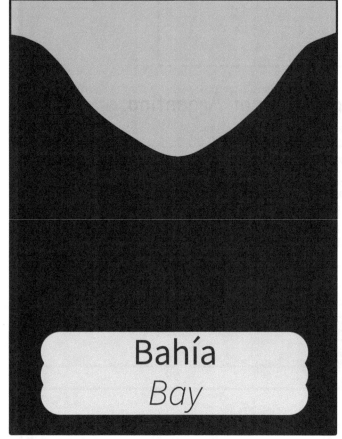

Bahía
Bay

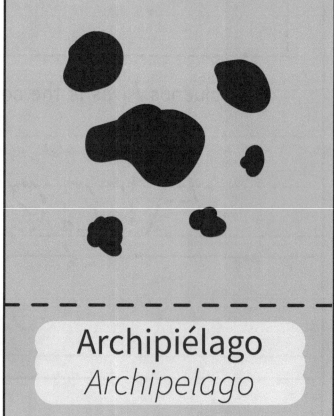

Archipiélago
Archipelago

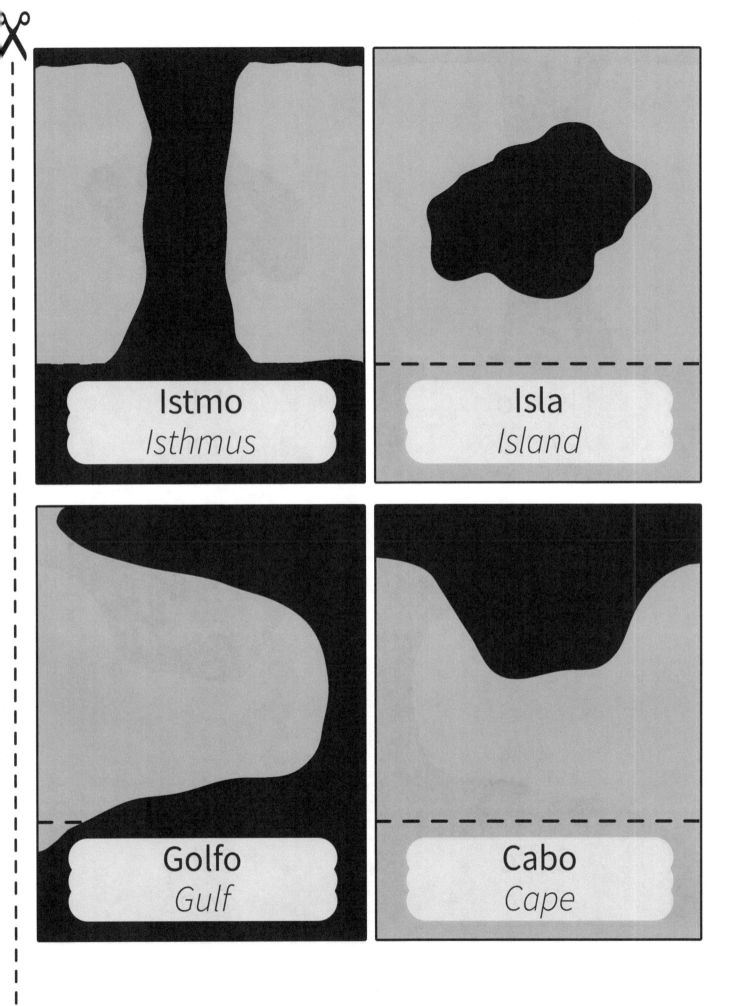

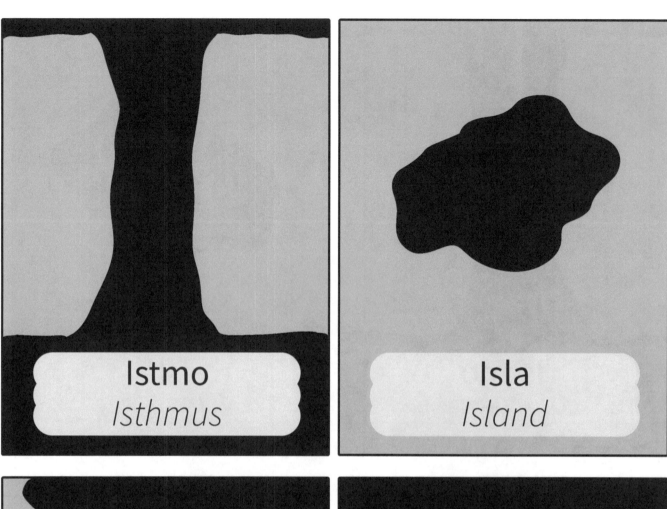
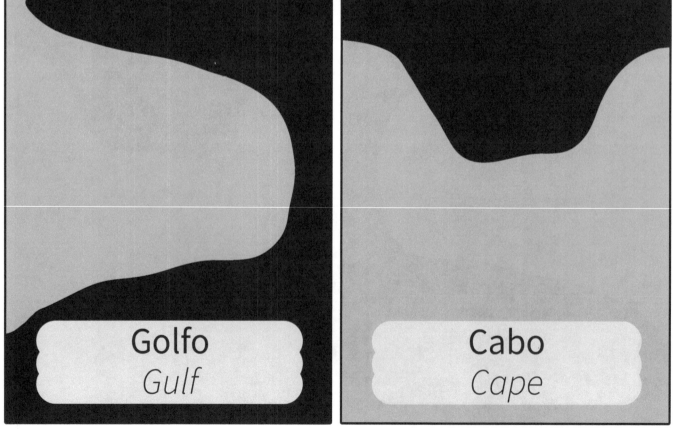

Sistema de Lagos
System of Lakes

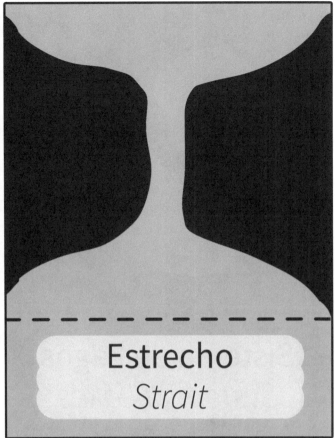

Estrecho
Strait

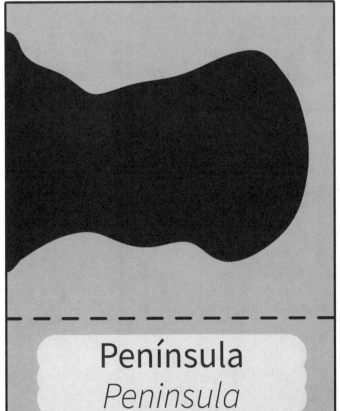

Península
Peninsula

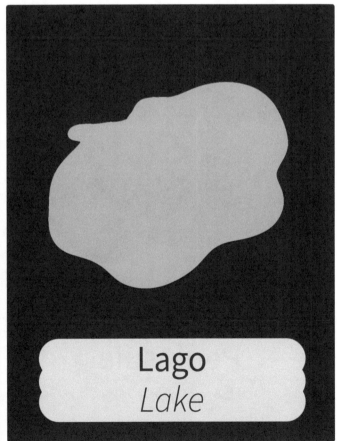

Lago
Lake

Sistema de Lagos
System of Lakes

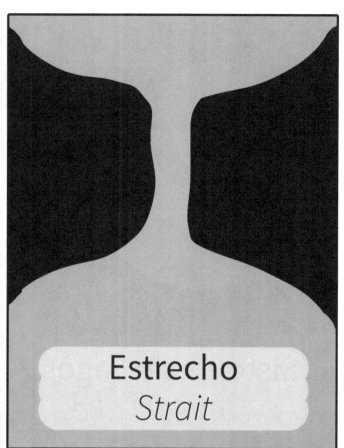

Estrecho
Strait

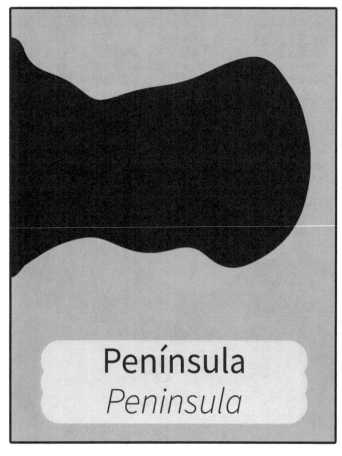

Península
Peninsula

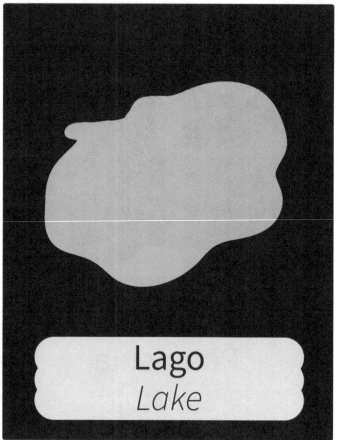

Lago
Lake

Name: _____ Date: _____

Spanish First Words & Writing Practice

Directions: Trace the word as shown and then try to write it on your own.

cold

Frío

Frío

Frío

Write out the word:

Name: _____ Date: _____

Spanish First Words & Writing Practice

Directions: Trace the word as shown and then try to write it on your own.

cat

Gato

Write out the word:

Name: _____ Date: _____

Spanish First Words & Writing Practice

Directions: Trace the word as shown and then try to write it on your own.

cheese

Queso

Write out the word:

Name: _____ Date: _____

Spanish First Words & Writing Practice

Directions: Trace the word as shown and then try to write it on your own.

chick

Polluelo

Polluelo

Polluelo

Write out the word:

Name: _____ Date: _____

Spanish First Words & Writing Practice

Directions: Trace the word as shown and then try to write it on your own.

chicken

Gallina

Gallina

Gallina

Write out the word:

Name: _____ Date: _____

Spanish First Words & Writing Practice

Directions: Trace the word as shown and then try to write it on your own.

circle

Círculo

Círculo

Círculo

Write out the word:

Name: _____ Date: _____

Spanish First Words & Writing Practice

Directions: Trace the word as shown and then try to write it on your own.

COW

Vaca

Vaca

Vaca

Write out the word:

Name: _____ Date: _____

Spanish First Words & Writing Practice

Directions: Trace the word as shown and then try to write it on your own.

daddy

Papi

Write out the word:

Name: _____ Date: _____

Spanish First Words & Writing Practice

Directions: Trace the word as shown and then try to write it on your own.

dog

Perro

Perro

Perro

Write out the word:

Name: _____ Date: _____

Spanish First Words & Writing Practice

Directions: Trace the word as shown and then try to write it on your own.

dolphin

Delfín

Write out the word:

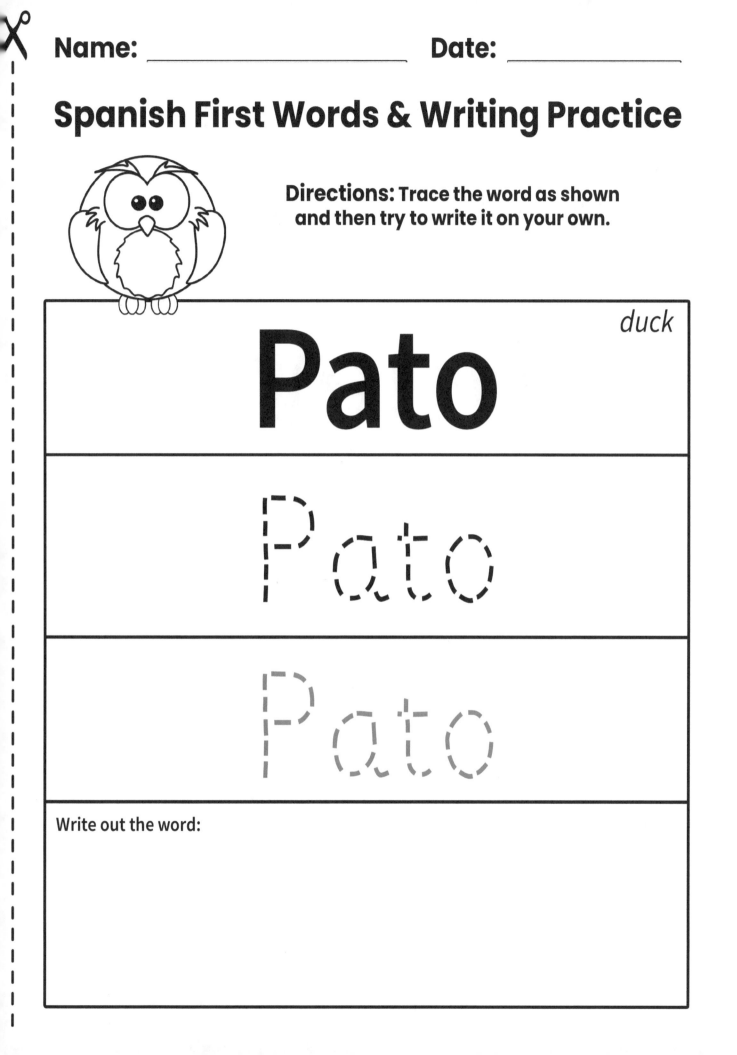

Name: _____ Date: _____

Spanish First Words & Writing Practice

Directions: Trace the word as shown and then try to write it on your own.

egg

Huevo

Write out the word:

NETUNO
NEPTUNE

SATURNO
SATURN

URANO
URANUS

MARTE
MARS

JÚPITER
JUPITER

VENUS
VENUS

TIERRA
EARTH

MERCURIO
MERCURY

SOL
SUN

EL SISTEMA SOLAR
THE SOLAR SYSTEM

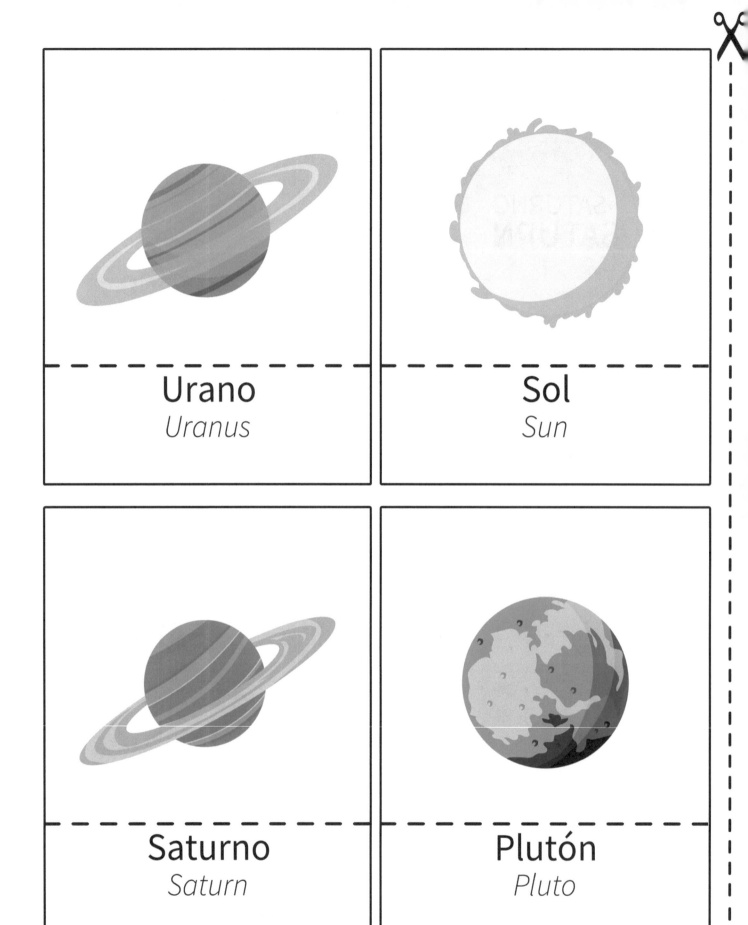

Urano	Sol
Uranus	*Sun*

Saturno	Plutón
Saturn	*Pluto*

Urano
Uranus

Sol
Sun

Saturno
Saturn

Plutón
Pluto

Mercurio
Mercury

Marte
Mars

Júpiter
Jupiter

Neptuno
Neptune

Tierra
Earth

Cometa
Comet

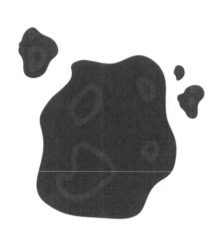

Asteroides
Asteroids

Venus
Venus

Tierra
Earth

Cometa
Comet

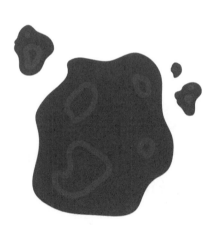

Asteroides
Asteroids

Venus
Venus

Thank you for learning with us!

Choosing to teach your child at home can sometimes be a difficult decision for the family financially.

If you know a family in need that would love this book, please send me an email.

I will send you a PDF of this book with no questions asked.

doodlesafari@gmail.com

Made in United States
Troutdale, OR
12/10/2023

15631735R10064